Real Food

Food

FOR
Cats

Real Food FOR Cats

50 Vet-Approved Recipes to Please the Feline Gastronome

By Patti Delmonte
Illustrated by Anne Davis

Storey Publishing

The mission of Storey Publishing is to serve our customers by publishing practical information that encourages personal independence in harmony with the environment.

Edited by Nancy W. Ringer and Larry Shea
Cover design and art direction by Meredith Maker
Illustrations © Anne Davis
Text design by Kathy Herlihy-Paoli
Text production by Erin Lincourt and Jennifer Jepson Smith
Many thanks to Veterinary Nutritional Consultations and Roger Valentine, D.V.M.,
    for reviewing the manuscript and recipes.

Printed in the United States by Malloy
10 9 8 7

Library of Congress Cataloging-in-Publication Data

Delmonte, Patti.
  Real food for cats: 50 vet-approved recipes to please the feline gastronome / by
  Patti Delmonte. — rev. ed.
      p. cm.
  Includes index.
  ISBN 978-1-58017-409-1 (alk. paper)
  1. Cats—Food—Recipes. I. Title.
SF447.6 .D45 2001
636.8'0855—dc21   2001049087

DEDICATION

To my husband Tom — thank you for
sharing your life with me.

To my sons, Joshua and Sean — two thankful hearts and tender spirits.
I am pleased that the young men you are becoming
will be a blessing and honor to our Heavenly Father.

ACKNOWLEDGMENTS

I want to thank Dr. David S. Kronfeld for his patience, his insights, and his enthusiasm. The vast amount of research material that he provided proved invaluable toward the goal of creating a nutritionally credible cookbook for cats.

I am grateful to Dr. L. D. Lewis and Dr. Mark L. Morris for permission to reprint their special diet recipes (see pages 99–113) from their book *Small Animal Clinical Nutrition.*

And thank you to the Lord of Creation, who created everything, especially cats.

CONTENTS

HOOF

Beef or Pork with Bean Sprouts ▪ Lamb Stew ▪ Kidney Stew
"Hearty" Beef ▪ Kitty-Size Lasagna ▪ Kitty Pizza ▪ Beef and
Bean Sauté ▪ Kitty Taco ▪ Kitty Cheeseburger ▪ Mews and
Purrs Meat Loaf

EGGS, CHEESE, AND MORE

Western Scramble for Kitty Roundups ▪ Kitty on the Run
Cheese Scramble ▪ Kitty Fondue ▪ Grassy Goodness
Purr-Fect Pasta

TANDEM COOKING

Beef Stroganoff ▪ Shish Kebab ▪ Chicken Paprika
Salmon Loaf ▪ Rabbit Stew ▪ Chicken Cordon Bleu

SPECIAL DIETS

Allergy Diet ▪ Soft, Bland Diet ▪ Reducing Diet
Feline Kidney Diet ▪ Restricted Mineral Diet

FOREWORD

Reciprocation is the basis of our relationship with cats. We have selected their species as companions for our own pleasure, and hopefully they enjoy us in the same way.

Our impositions on their nature have taken away from cats the primitive ability to make choices for their own personal welfare. We now make some, though by no means all, important decisions in their lives. One of the main choices that a cat owner faces is the diet that will be best for his or her pet. This book offers gastronomic pleasures: recipes that work, are balanced nutritionally, are palatable for cats, and are fun for us to cook.

These recipes represent an alternative to commercial cat food. Proprietary pet foods are a triumph of technology: They are processed to convert the unused by-products of human food (essentially "non-food" for humans) into food for pets. By contrast, the inspired recipes in this book use real human food as a basis for nutritious and delicious food for cats.

Today's cat remains an obligatory carnivore, locked in the past. The cat's biochemistry and behavior fall into patterns much narrower than those of its evolutionary cousin, the dog. The cat's avid penchant for animal protein, for instance, reflects the inability of its liver to regulate the breakdown of amino acids. Most animals have this conserving ability, but the cat's fore-bears never needed it because their diet contained plenty of protein. The cat also remains attached to a number of specific dietary requirements for vitamins such as retinol and niacin, and for amino acids such as arginine.

The cat does *not* thrive on diets used to feed dogs. So if one wishes to cook for cats, one must take care, exceedingly good and enlightened care, to do it right. On special occasions, give your cat a break from her commercial food diet and treat her to any of the recipes in this book. To provide a balanced diet, however, you should not serve your cat one or two of the recipes here exclusively. Vary your cat's menu, combining a range of the recipes with meals of traditional cat food.

All of these recipes offer opportunities for pleasure and togetherness. As the Romans, who first domesticated cats to guard their granaries, used to say: *Symbiotica et sympatico hominum philapussicat est.**

Dr. David S. Kronfeld
Clark Professor of Nutrition
School of Veterinary Medicine
University of Pennsylvania

*Symbiotic and sympathetic
is the person who
loves pussycats.

INTRODUCTION

W hether you are trying out one of these recipes to reward your cat for catching that pesky mouse or because it just sounds like something new and fun to do, the purpose of this book is to offer you a fun collection of nutritional treats for your feline pal.

It is also my intent to provide you with enough knowledge of your pet's dietary needs that you can whip up any variety of nutritionally sound homemade treats on your own. Pay particular attention to the four supplements mentioned in Dr. Kronfeld's "Theme Recipe" on page 2: liver, corn oil, bonemeal, and iodized salt. These supplements help provide many of the vitamins, minerals, and fatty acids that are essential to your cat's diet. Also look at the assortment of tips, warnings, and suggestions throughout the book. These will provide you with additional information on nutrition, food preparation, ingredient substitutions, and other practical issues in feeding and caring for your cat.

One of my favorite sections of the book is the chapter on "tandem" recipes. These are simple recipes for "Real Food for People," but with only slight modifications you can make some portions suitable for your cat as well. However, people food is people food. Use these and the other recipes in this book only as treats for special occasions. If you want to feed your cat a completely homemade diet, you should consult with your veterinarian first. And no cat with a history of illness, such as feline lower urinary tract disease (F.L.U.T.D.), should be given a homemade meal without prior approval from your vet.

THE KRONFELD DIET FOR CATS

Over the years, many cat fanciers have asked the author of the foreword, Dr. David S. Kronfeld, how to cook for their cats. His "Theme Recipe" uses ground meat and rice as staples because they are important sources of energy. The supplements — liver, bonemeal, corn oil, and iodized salt — are designed to provide all of the essential nutrients not found in the staples in the most convenient way possible.

THE THEME RECIPE

1 cup water
⅓ cup dry rice (brown or white)
2 teaspoons corn oil
½ teaspoon iodized salt
⅔ cup ground meat
1 tablespoon bonemeal
2 tablespoons cooked liver
(see page 4 for instructions
on preparing liver)

1. Bring the water to a boil. Add the rice, corn oil, and salt, and simmer for 20 minutes over low heat.

2. Dredge the meat with the bonemeal. Add the meat and liver to the rice mixture, stir, and simmer for another 15 minutes.

3. Cool and serve. Leftovers should be refrigerated or frozen.

MAKES 3 SERVINGS

KEEP FOOD REFRIGERATED!

You don't leave your own Monday-night leftovers sitting around on the kitchen counter until Thursday, do you? Well, it's the same with the food you cook for your cat. Most of the recipes in this book provide anywhere from two to six servings. Be sure to label and date leftover portions and store them covered in the refrigerator as soon as you finish serving your kitty's dinner. Prepared recipes can be safely refrigerated for only three to four days, and portions should be frozen immediately if you intend to keep them for any longer period. Do not feed anything to your cat that has been in the refrigerator longer than four days or that smells at all suspect.

VARIATIONS ON A THEME

The meat used in Dr. Kronfeld's theme recipe is usually hamburger with a medium fat content. Fat cats may benefit from lean meat or an organ meat such as heart. You could also replace the meat in the recipe with fish. Some types of fish (salmon, for example) are fatty and others (such as flounder) are lean. Cats also love chicken, turkey, goose, and duck — all of which may replace hamburger. Rice can be replaced by barley, potato, canned or frozen corn, or tapioca. But rice is hard to beat for cats because it is easily digested and blends well with other foods.

Liver is needed to provide necessary trace minerals and vitamins. You may replace it with other organ meats, such as kidney or sweetbreads, but none have the potency and benefits of liver. The easiest way to cook liver is to chop it into very small (kitty-bite-size) pieces and then boil it for about 15 minutes. Be sure to drain it well.

Steamed bonemeal is a good source of calcium. It is sometimes available at health food and pet stores, but it can be difficult to find. If you can't lay your

hands on bonemeal, you can substitute calcium carbonate; crushed TUMS tablets and finely ground eggshells are good sources of calcium carbonate. Other good sources of calcium include milk and other dairy foods as well as green leafy vegetables.

Corn oil contains linoleic acid, an essential fatty acid proven beneficial to the health of cats. It may be replaced by wheat germ oil.

4

A FULL MEASURE OF CALCIUM

Calcium is absorbed less efficiently by cats when they are on a cereal diet. Soybeans, in particular, compound this problem because they contain an organic compound, phytin, that binds calcium to itself and further inhibits absorption.

Vegetable greens are high in calcium and can be chopped and added to most feline recipes. Some feline favorites include Swiss chard, collard greens, dandelion greens, kale, mustard greens, parsley, and spinach.

Bonemeal is an excellent source of calcium, but it can be hard to find. Calcium carbonate is the most readily available form of calcium that is palatable to cats. Ground eggshells and crushed TUMS tablets are good sources of calcium carbonate. If you use eggshells, take them only from hard-cooked eggs; shells from raw eggs can contain salmonella bacteria and can make your cat become ill.

TREATS

We give our dogs treats for fetching the newspaper, rolling over, chasing a stick, and even simply sitting down on command. Cats, of course, aspire to loftier heights. They understand commands — "Get DOWN from there!" — but usually obey only when you actually heave yourself up from your comfortable seat on the sofa and approach the forbidden countertop with heavy footsteps. When you are just a step or two away from physically removing Fluffy from her perch, she nonchalantly hops down, satisfied that you do indeed mean what you say.

We humans are well trained.

But that's not to say that you can't train a cat to obey commands or that you shouldn't reward a cat for good behavior, or even just for being adorable. The recipes in this chapter yield scrumptious cookies, kibble, and other treats irresistible to our furry friends. Use them to reward your cat for obeying a command or to tempt a cat out from underneath the bed when it's time for a trip to the vet — or just on general principle, knowing that in the natural order of things, cats are meant to be pampered.

Reserve a special word or phrase to signal to your cat that it's time for a treat. As all cat owners know well, cats understand human language; they simply choose to ignore it most of the time. But it won't take long for your cat to realize that THIS particular word means YUM! She'll scramble to your side as fast as her paws can carry her upon hearing that magic call, "Who wants a treat?"

TABBY TUNA POPSICLES

When the heat of summer hits, help your feline friend cool down with this fine, fishy treat. It packs a hit of a cat's favorite spice: catnip.

> 1 6-ounce can of water-packed tuna
> 1 teaspoon organic catnip, crushed fine

1. Drain the liquid from the tuna into a cup with a pouring spout.

2. Fill each compartment of a plastic ice cube tray halfway with water.

3. Lightly sprinkle catnip into each compartment.

4. Fill the rest of the ice cube tray with the tuna water.

5. Place the tray in the freezer and allow the cubes to freeze solid.

6. Serve one of these tuna popsicles in your cat's bowl.

MAKES 14 TO 16 SERVINGS

MEOW-VA-LOUS MACKEREL MUNCHIES

The next time your cat does her "peticure" on the scratching post and not on the arm of your sofa, reward her with a few of these healthy homemade treats.

> ½ cup canned mackerel, drained
> 1 egg, beaten
> 1 cup bread crumbs
> 1 teaspoon brewer's yeast

1. Preheat oven to 350°F.

2. Place all the ingredients in a medium-sized bowl.

3. Mix the ingredients using a fork.

4. Form the mix into balls about the size of marbles and drop them onto a greased cookie sheet about one inch apart.

5. Bake for 7 to 8 minutes, or until the balls are golden and crispy.

6. Allow to cool before serving. Store the extra treats in an airtight container in the refrigerator.

MAKES 8 SERVINGS

MMMM MEATY COOKIES
* * * *

You may prefer a sweet treat, but your kitty craves a meat treat. Pamper your cat by serving this sensational snack.

> ½ cup wheat germ
> ½ cup dry milk
> 1 teaspoon honey
> 1 small jar of beef puree baby food

1. Preheat oven to 350°F.

2. With a wooden spoon, stir together the wheat germ, dry milk, and honey in a small mixing bowl.

3. Add the beef puree and stir until thoroughly mixed.

4. Form the mixture into small balls.

5. Place the balls on a greased cookie sheet and flatten them with a fork.

6. Bake 8 to 10 minutes.

7. Cool before serving. Store the leftovers in an airtight container in the refrigerator.

MAKES 8 TO 10 SERVINGS

TROUT TREATS
✳ ✳ ✳ ✳

Your cat will signal her paw-si-tively pleasing approval if you break from the monotony of store-bought treats by serving these homemade yum-yums.

> 1 tablespoon vegetable oil
> 2 egg yolks
> 1 small trout filet, baked
> 4 tablespoons instant oatmeal

1. Preheat oven to 350°F.

2. Coat a baking pan with the vegetable oil.

3. In a small bowl, whisk the egg yolks.

4. Dip the trout in the egg mix and then coat the fish with oatmeal.

5. Place the coated fish in the pan and bake for 15 to 18 minutes.

6. Allow to cool and then cut into half-inch pieces.

MAKES 6 TO
8 SERVINGS

CAT CHOW COOKIES

♡♡♡♡♡

Celebrate your cat's birthday or other special occasion not by baking a cake, but by making these tasty cookies. Your cat will clamor for more!

1 cup wheat flour
¼ cup soy flour
¼ cup milk
⅓ cup powdered milk
1 egg
2 tablespoons wheat germ
2 tablespoons molasses
2 tablespoons margarine
1 teaspoon organic catnip

1. Preheat oven to 350°F.

2. In a large mixing bowl, stir together all the ingredients.

3. Lightly flour a rolling pin. Roll out the batter on a greased cookie sheet.

4. Cut into half-inch pieces.

5. Bake for 20 to 22 minutes.

6. Allow to cool before serving. Store the leftovers in an airtight container in a cool place.

MAKES 6 TO 8 SERVINGS

FIN

ats love fish like fish love water. They can't resist it, and if you have it in the house, they'll convince you that they absolutely can't live without it. Open a can of tuna fish in the kitchen and — zoom! — cats appear panting at your feet, begging shamelessly for a bite. They wind about your ankles, meow anxiously, look pitiful, and, if you turn your back for a second, will snatch a bite and scamper out of the room lickety-split.

Fish makes a wonderfully nutritious meal for felines. It is rich in essential nutrients, including iodine and zinc. Fatty fish such as salmon, tuna, mackerel, herring, and whitefish are rich in vitamins A and D and are a good source of protein.

If your cat is on a weight reduction diet, lean fish is a good meal choice. Cod, haddock, flounder, and bass are lean fish; in fact, they are far leaner than the leanest meat.

Some fish contain an enzyme that reduces the ability to absorb thiamine, a vitamin that is essential to normal metabolism and nerve function. This enzyme, thiaminase, is destroyed by the cooking process. Therefore, it is a good idea to cook all fish prior to serving.

YOU GOTTA HAVE SOLE

Noodles and a cheesy sauce help make this dish a must-have meal.

- ½ pound fillet of sole
- 2 tablespoons chopped parsley
- Salt and pepper
- 1 tablespoon butter
- 1 tablespoon flour
- ¼ cup milk
- ¼ cup grated cheddar cheese
- 2 tablespoons cooked liver
  (see page 4 for instructions)
- ½ teaspoon iodized salt
- ⅔ cup cooked noodles, cut into
  kitty-bite-size pieces (or cooked rice)

1. Preheat oven to 450°F.

2. Put the sole in a small, greased baking dish. Sprinkle with parsley and a dash of salt and pepper. Add enough water to just cover the bottom of the dish.

3. Cook for 10 minutes. Remove from the oven, cool, and cut into small pieces.

4. Melt the butter in a small saucepan. Stir in the flour and heat until bubbling. Gradually stir in the milk and cook, stirring constantly, until the mixture thickens. Add the cheese, liver, and salt; stir until the cheese has melted. DO NOT BOIL.

5. Add the chopped fish and the noodles to the cheese sauce and stir well. Cool and serve.

MAKES 4 TO 6 SERVINGS

18

KITTY JAMBALAYA

This New Orleans–inspired feast — loaded with beef, chicken, and seafood — is sure to include a few of your cat's favorite things.

⅓ cup ground beef
1 clove garlic, finely chopped
¼ cup diced tomato
⅔ cup uncooked rice
⅓ cup chopped chicken
⅓ cup chopped shrimp
⅓ cup *boned* and chopped fish
2 cups water
2 teaspoons corn oil
2 teaspoons bonemeal
2 tablespoons cooked liver (see page 4 for instructions)
1 teaspoon iodized salt

1. Sauté the ground beef in a medium-sized saucepan. Remove the meat from the pan. Add the garlic to the pan and sauté briefly.

2. Add the tomato and rice; stir-fry until the tomato is warmed through. Add the rest of the ingredients and stir. Cover and simmer for 15 minutes. Stir the mixture to blend the ingredients and simmer for 10 more minutes. Let cool, then serve.

MAKES 5 OR 6 SERVINGS

TUNA CAKES

(ats will race even faster to the sound of a whirring can opener if they think you're about to prepare this tasty and nutritious dish.

> 2 eggs
> 1 6-ounce can tuna, drained and flaked
> 4 slices bread, cubed into kitty-bite-size pieces
> ½ teaspoon iodized salt
> 1 teaspoon brewer's yeast
> 1 teaspoon bonemeal
> 2 tablespoons margarine

1. Beat the eggs lightly in a bowl. Add the tuna, bread cubes, salt, brewer's yeast, and bonemeal. Mix thoroughly until moistened.

2. Form into small patties. Melt the margarine in a skillet and fry the patties until golden brown. When cool, crumble each patty and serve.

MAKES 3 TO 5 SERVINGS

FISH FEASTS

Even the slightest fishy aroma will give your cat pleasant dreams of snapping up every last morsel she can get her paws on. Just make certain that any fish that you serve (or that your cat can get on her own) is free of bones. Bones can cause your cat to choke or can even damage a cat's digestive tract. It's essential that you keep fish, chicken, and other bones out of your pet's reach. Make sure that your garbage cans have secure, cat-proof lids; when it comes to something fishy-smelling, a cat can be as ingenious as a wily raccoon in getting into the garbage.

SARDINES AND RICE (KITTY HEAVEN)

♡♡♡♡♡

Here's a meal that's quick and easy to make when you have some leftover rice in the refrigerator and a few cans of sardines in the cupboard.

 2 flat cans of sardines in oil
 ⅔ cup cooked rice
 1 tablespoon cooked liver (see
    page 4 for instructions)
 ¼ cup chopped parsley

1. Combine all the ingredients in a mixing bowl. Use a wooden spoon to stir and break up the sardines into kitty-bite-size pieces. Serve immediately.

2. Store unused portions in an airtight container in the refrigerator.

MAKES 2 OR
3 SERVINGS

sardines

24

FISH CHOWDER

This hearty meal could be made with a lean fish, such as cod, or with a fattier fish, such as salmon.

½ pound fish, *boned* and cut into
  kitty-bite-size pieces
1 cup creamed corn
¼ cup finely chopped potato
1 clove garlic, minced
1 tablespoon margarine
1 cup milk
1 tablespoon cooked liver (see
  page 4 for instructions)
½ teaspoon iodized salt
Grated cheese (optional)

1. Combine all the ingredients in a medium-sized saucepan. Cover and simmer for 20 minutes.

2. Cool and serve plain or topped with grated cheese.

MAKES 4 OR 5 SERVINGS

25

MEOWSHI SUSHI

(ats knew the delight of eating sushi long before it became trendy; here a can of tuna makes an easy source of fish.

⅓ cup uncooked rice
⅔ cup chicken broth
1 teaspoon corn oil
⅓ cup grated carrot
1 6-ounce can tuna, drained and flaked
½ teaspoon brewer's yeast

1. Combine the rice with the chicken broth and corn oil in a pot and bring to a boil. After about 15 minutes, but *before* all the liquid is absorbed, add the grated carrot. When the liquid is absorbed and the rice is cooked, set aside.

2. When the rice has cooled, mix in the flaked tuna. Sprinkle with brewer's yeast just before serving.

MAKES 2 OR 3 SERVINGS

26

BOOGALOO SHRIMP

Shrimp makes a tasty special treat to add to your cat's diet. Combined here with rice and a creamy sauce, it is likely to become one of your cat's favorites.

¼ pound shrimp, cooked
  and shelled
1 tablespoon margarine
¼ cup sour cream
½ teaspoon iodized salt
1 teaspoon brewer's yeast
⅔ cup cooked rice

1. In a nonstick saucepan, sauté the shrimp in the margarine until heated through. Then remove from heat.

2. Stir in the sour cream, salt, and brewer's yeast. When the mixture is cool, combine with the cooked rice and serve. Store unused portions in an airtight container in the refrigerator.

MAKES 2 OR 3 SERVINGS

FABULOUS FiSH TACOS
✳ ✳ ✳ ✳

Your kitty will feel like navigating the seven seas in search of more international cuisine after she devours this terrific taco entrée.

> 2 ounces cooked cod, chopped fine
> 2 tablespoons chicken broth
> 2 tablespoons sour cream
> 1 teaspoon salt
> 1 flour tortilla

1. Place the cod in a microwave-safe bowl with a little water. Steam the cod in the microwave oven on HIGH for 2 minutes.

2. In a medium-sized bowl, blend the chicken broth, sour cream, salt, and cod.

3. Lay out a flour tortilla and spoon the fish mix onto it.

4. Roll the filled tortilla and pinch the ends closed. Cut the tortilla into half-inch pieces.

5. Allow the fish to cool before serving this to your cat.

MAKES 1 SERVING

SENSATIONAL SARDINE SOUP
* * * *

Sardines are greasy, smelly, and crunchy — just what your cat craves! You may turn up your nose, but your cat will be meowing for second helpings.

- 2 canned sardines
- 1 tablespoon margarine
- 1 cup water
- ¼ cup steamed and finely chopped zucchini

1. Sauté the sardines in the margarine in a small frying pan over medium heat.

2. Add the water and zucchini after the margarine has completely melted.

3. Bring to a boil and then remove from the stove.

4. Mash the sardines.

5. Allow to cool before serving.

MAKES 1 SERVING

FEATHER

ell, we're not talking parakeets and cockatoos here. We're also not going to discuss robins, chickadees, sparrows, and other wild birds, although your crafty feline hunter might like to. Keep your feathered friends well guarded from your furry feline friends, and instead hand out liberal rations of Chicken Salad, Turkey Surprise, and the other bird-based recipes in this chapter. A happy, harmonious household shall reign forevermore.

It is of the utmost importance that you remove all bones from poultry meat before serving it to your cat. Chicken bones (and those of other poultry meats) tend to be thin and fragile; they splinter when chewed and, if swallowed, can cause internal bleeding and other damage. Knowing the persistence of a cat that smells chicken, I recommend that you bag up the chicken bones immediately upon removing them and dispose of them, outdoors, in a sturdy, raccoon-proof (and thus cat-proof) garbage can. In addition, never leave chicken unattended in your kitchen or on your plate. In one second, thump!, the cat's on the table; two seconds, thump-thump!, cat and chicken have hit the floor; and three seconds, whooosh!, cat and bird have disappeared round the corner, a blur of delighted fur streaking for the nearest safe hiding place.

You don't need much meat to concoct these recipes; they are useful ways to use up leftovers while also endearing you to your cat. So pull out the chopping block and get ready to cook — and try not to trip over that everloving bundle of feline joy winding itself around your ankles.

(HiCKEN WiTH GREENS

Beet greens are a nutritional powerhouse, packed with vitamins and minerals. However, some cats' digestive systems are somewhat sensitive to beets and to greens in general. You may want to introduce your cat gradually to greens before using the full amount given here.

⅔ cup chicken with giblets (especially the liver)
1 cup tomato juice, or ½ cup tomato puree and ½ cup water
⅓ cup uncooked rice
½ cup finely chopped beet greens
1 clove garlic, minced
½ teaspoon iodized salt
1 teaspoon corn oil

1. Cut the chicken and giblets into kitty-bite-size pieces.

2. Bring the tomato juice to a low boil in a saucepan. Add the chicken and rice, cover, and simmer for 15 minutes. Add the greens, garlic, and salt. Cover and simmer for another 10 minutes.

3. Remove from heat and stir in the corn oil. Cool before serving.

MAKES 2 OR 3 SERVINGS

CHICKEN SALAD

When the weather next turns warm and sunny, why not take your cat and this picnic favorite outside for a meal in the great outdoors?

   1 tablespoon corn oil
   1 tablespoon finely chopped celery
   1 tablespoon finely chopped bell pepper
   ⅓ cup cooked, chopped chicken
   2 tablespoons ricotta cheese
   2 tablespoons plain yogurt or sour cream
   ½ teaspoon iodized salt
   1 teaspoon brewer's yeast
   ¼ cup chopped sprouts

1. Heat the oil in a skillet. Add the celery and bell pepper and cook until soft. Let the vegetables cool.

2. In a mixing bowl, combine the rest of the ingredients, except for the sprouts, and mix well. Stir in the cooled vegetables. Top with the sprouts and serve.

MAKES 2 OR 3 SERVINGS

CHICKEN CHOW MEIN

Chow mein (it means "fried noodles") was actually first served in American Chinese restaurants. Your cat, however, won't care one whisker about its cultural authenticity, because this kitty version is delicious!

2 tablespoons corn oil
¼ cup finely chopped green pepper
¼ cup finely chopped red pepper
1 tablespoon flour
2 teaspoons bonemeal
½ cup chicken broth
1 tablespoon soy sauce
½ teaspoon iodized salt
Dash of pepper
¼ cup finely chopped mushrooms
½ pound chicken breast, cooked and chopped
2 tablespoons cooked liver (see page 4 for instructions)
1½ cups cooked egg noodles, chopped

1. Heat the corn oil in a saucepan. Add the green pepper and red pepper; sauté until the peppers are soft. Sprinkle with flour and bonemeal.

2. Gradually stir in the chicken broth. Cover and simmer for 10 minutes. Add the soy sauce, the salt, a dash of pepper, the mushrooms, the chicken, and the liver. Simmer another 10 minutes.

3. Remove from heat and stir in the noodles. Cool and serve.

MAKES 4 TO 6 SERVINGS

36

GIZZARD GOULASH

The name may sound a bit like Halloween fare, but this is a good way to put those chicken innards to a nutritious use.

- 1 tablespoon corn oil
- ½ pound chicken gizzards and/or hearts chopped into kitty-bite-size pieces
- 1 clove garlic, minced
- ½ teaspoon paprika
- ½ teaspoon iodized salt
- 1 medium tomato, chopped fine
- 1 tablespoon cooked liver (see page 4 for instructions)
- 1 cup cooked macaroni noodles, chopped into kitty-bite-size pieces
- ¼ cup sour cream

1. Heat the oil in a skillet. Add the chicken gizzards and lightly brown.

2. Add the garlic to the skillet and sauté for about 3 minutes. Blend in the paprika and salt.

3. Add the tomato and liver and cook 3 to 5 minutes, stirring constantly, until the tomato has become soft and runny.

4. Remove from heat; stir in the noodles and sour cream. Cool and serve.

MAKES 3 TO 5 SERVINGS

GIVING THE BRUSH-OFF TO HAIR BALLS

A hair ball is an accumulation of hair in a cat's stomach as a result of his or her own grooming. Hairballs can occur even if you brush your pet regularly. Symptoms are a dry cough, vomiting after meals, and constipation. You can help your cat eliminate hair balls by applying a dab of petroleum jelly to the end of his or her nose; once the cat licks it off, it will serve as an internal lubricant.

Combing is the best way to prevent hair balls. Longhaired cats need a combing two or three times a week; for shorthaired cats, once a week is fine.

The natural shedding seasons for cats are the spring and, to a lesser degree, the fall. Cats may also shed because of stress (illness, moving, owner's vacation) or because of dry indoor heat used during the winter months. During the shedding season, try to schedule a few extra grooming sessions.

If yours is an indoor cat, you can help prevent hair balls by making a little pot of grass available. Keep the grass pot in a place that your cat frequents: by a sliding glass door or on a favorite windowsill. Just make it accessible to your cat for occasional nibbling.

Grass and other vegetable matter are fibrous and are not easily digested by cats. These fibrous materials tend to absorb water, expand, and soften, which provides bulk in the digestive tract. This helps carry hair and other residues out in the feces.

CHICKEN SOUP

▽△▽△▽△▽

Chicken soup is comfort food for humans and felines alike. If your cat has had a tough day — a trip to the vet, contractors making a racket in the house, or even a dearth of bugs for your proud hunter to chase — cheer him up with this soothing soup.

- ½ cup lentils
- 2 cups water
- 2 chicken breasts, boned and cut into kitty-bite-size pieces
- ¼ cup finely chopped carrot
- ¼ cup finely chopped broccoli
- 1 clove garlic, minced
- 1 teaspoon iodized salt
- 2 teaspoons bonemeal
- 2 tablespoons corn oil
- 2 tablespoons liver (cooked or raw)

1. Place the lentils in a 2-quart pan, add the water, and bring to a boil. Lower the heat, cover, and simmer for 30 minutes.

2. Add the remaining ingredients to the pan and simmer another 15 to 20 minutes, stirring occasionally.

3. Cool and serve by itself or over dry food. (Note: If your cat sometimes just picks out his or her favorite flavors, process a portion of the recipe in the blender on a low setting for a few seconds to create a finer consistency.)

MAKES 4 OR 5 SERVINGS

CHICKEN AND ASPARAGUS CASSEROLE

Most cats enjoy nibbling on cooked asparagus. It can be stringy, though, so be sure to peel it and chop it finely to make it easier for your cat to eat.

⅔ cup cooked, boned, and chopped chicken
⅔ cup cooked elbow macaroni (small size)
1 stalk asparagus, chopped fine
1 tablespoon chopped, cooked liver
   (see page 4 for instructions)
2 tablespoons milk
2 tablespoons ricotta or cottage cheese
1 teaspoon corn oil
½ teaspoon iodized salt
2 tablespoons grated cheddar or white cheese

1. Preheat oven to 375°F.

2. Combine all the ingredients except the grated cheese in a medium-sized mixing bowl and stir to blend.

3. Put the mixture in a small, well-greased casserole or small glass bread pan and top with grated cheese. Bake for 20 minutes. Cool and serve.

MAKES 3 OR 4 SERVINGS

TURKEY SURPRISE

Turkey won't be much of a surprise to the people at your Thanksgiving table, but your cat will be delighted to see this dish in her bowl on that holiday — or any other day, for that matter.

> 1 teaspoon iodized salt
> 2 teaspoons corn oil
> 1½ cups water
> ½ cup uncooked rice
> ½ pound turkey giblets, chopped into kitty-bite-size pieces
> ¼ cup finely chopped carrot
> ½ cup chopped spinach

1. Add the salt and oil to the water and bring to a boil. Pour the rice into the boiling water, lower heat, cover, and cook for 10 minutes.

2. Stir in the turkey giblets, carrot, and spinach. Cover and simmer over low heat for another 10 minutes. Cool and serve.

MAKES 4 OR 5 SERVINGS

43

HEAVENLY TURKEY LEFTOVERS
✳ ✳ ✳ ✳

Need some help eating the leftover turkey from Thanksgiving? Allow your cat to help. This tasty recipe provides purr-fect nutritional goodness that will make your cat feel like the holiday meal was prepared just for him.

> 1 cup cooked, diced turkey
> ¼ cup steamed and finely diced carrots
> ¼ cup steamed and finely diced broccoli
> ½ cup chicken broth
> 2 teaspoons brewer's yeast
> ½ teaspoon garlic powder

1. In a medium-sized bowl, thoroughly mix all the ingredients.

2. Allow to cool before serving to your cat.

MAKES 2 OR 3 SERVINGS

HOOF

Kitty cheeseburger? Can a cheeseburger possibly be a healthy meal for a cat? You bet it is. Especially when it's made of broiled ground beef mixed with whole wheat bread crumbs and steamed carrots, all topped with mozzarella cheese. Sound good? It is. In fact, you just might want to try one yourself.

Beef, pork, lamb, and other meats "on the hoof," so to speak, are filled with the protein that cats need and crave. They are flavorful and easy to cook with, and most cats will dive right into dishes prepared with them. Mixed with vegetables; seasonings; and rice, bread, or grains, they make a taste-tempting, palate-pleasing, soul-satisfying meal that your cat will savor with great glee.

Many of the recipes in this chapter call for ground beef, which generally has a medium fat content. If your cat is on the chubby side, he may benefit from leaner cuts of beef, organ meats, fish, or poultry; just use these leaner meats in place of the ground beef.

As when cooking for humans, it is important that you cook all meats thoroughly before feeding them to your cat; cooking kills the bacteria often found in raw meats and safeguards your cat's health. In addition, be sure to carefully wash your cutting boards, all utensils, and your hands with hot water and soap after handling raw meat. If, lured into the kitchen by the aroma of a homemade meal, your cat is begging for attention, he'll just have to wait!

BEEF OR PORK WITH BEAN SPROUTS

My cat hungrily eyes the container every time I bring home Chinese takeout. Here's a similar dish just for felines.

- ½ pound ground beef or pork
- 1 tablespoon soy sauce
- 1 clove garlic, minced
- 1 tablespoon corn oil
- ¼ cup green beans, cut into kitty-bite-size pieces
- ¼ cup finely chopped mushrooms
- ½ cup finely chopped bean sprouts
- 1 teaspoon cornstarch
- ¼ cup chicken broth
- ½ teaspoon iodized salt
- ½–1 cup cooked rice
- 2 tablespoons cooked liver (see page 4 for instructions)
- 2 teaspoons bonemeal

1. Mix the meat with the soy sauce and garlic; marinate for at least 20 minutes.

2. Heat the oil in a skillet. Add the meat mixture and lightly brown. Add the green beans and sauté about 2 minutes. Add the mushrooms and sauté another 2 minutes. Add the bean sprouts and sauté 2 more minutes.

3. Mix the cornstarch with the chicken broth in a bowl. Add to the skillet and heat until the sauce has thickened; stir in the salt.

4. Remove from the heat and stir in the rice, liver, and bonemeal. Cool and serve.

MAKES 4 TO 6 SERVINGS

LAMB STEW

Your cat will rush into the kitchen like a lion if he knows you're bringing out this lamb dish.

- 1 tablespoon corn oil
- ½ pound boneless lamb, cut into kitty-bite-size pieces
- 3 tablespoons flour with a dash of salt
- 1 clove garlic, minced
- 1½ cups water
- ½ teaspoon iodized salt
- Pinch of basil
- 1 small carrot, minced
- ¼ cup peas, frozen or fresh (slightly mashed if needed)
- ½ cup corn kernels
- ½ cup chopped potato
- 2 teaspoons bonemeal
- ¼ cup cooked liver (see page 4 for instructions)

1. Heat the oil in a medium-sized saucepan. Dredge the lamb in the flour and add to the skillet. Lightly brown lamb on all sides.

2. Add the garlic to the skillet and sauté another minute. Add the water, salt, and basil. Cover and simmer 15 minutes.

3. Add the remaining ingredients. Cover and simmer approximately 15 minutes, or until the potatoes and carrots are done. Cool and serve.

MAKES 4 TO 6 SERVINGS

KIDNEY STEW

In England, with its beef and kidney pies, this dish might be more familiar. Here it makes an unusual but delicious and nutritious meal.

  1 tablespoon corn oil
  1 teaspoon iodized salt
  1½ cups water
  ½ pound beef kidney, cut into
      kitty-bite-size pieces
  ½ cup uncooked rice
  1 carrot, chopped fine
  4 mushrooms, chopped fine
  2 tablespoons tomato paste
  1 teaspoon bonemeal

1. Place the corn oil and salt in the water and bring to a boil.

2. Add the kidney, rice, carrot, mushrooms, and tomato paste to the boiling water. Cover and simmer over low heat for 20 minutes.

3. Remove from heat and stir in the bonemeal. Cool and serve.

MAKES 4 TO 6 SERVINGS

The starch in cereals tends to inhibit the efficient assimilation of food energy, protein, calcium, iron, zinc, and copper. Therefore, recipes that are high in cereal need to have liver, bonemeal, iodized salt, and corn oil added to give your cat a well-rounded meal.

"HEARTY" BEEF

♡ ♡ ♡ ♡ ♡

Beef heart isn't a familiar cut of meat for most of us, but it makes a fine protein source for your cat.

- ½ pound beef heart
- 1 tablespoon corn oil
- 1 clove garlic, minced
- ¼ cup finely chopped spinach
- 2 eggs
- ¼ cup cornmeal
- ½ teaspoon iodized salt
- 2 tablespoons cooked liver (see page 4 for instructions)

1. To prepare the beef heart, boil for 15 to 20 minutes. Let cool and chop into kitty-bite-size pieces.

2. Heat the corn oil in a skillet. Add the garlic and sauté briefly (30 seconds). Add the spinach and sauté for about a minute.

3. Beat the eggs in a medium-sized mixing bowl. Blend the cornmeal and salt with the eggs. Mix in the beef and liver. Add the mixture to the skillet and stir well; continue to cook until the eggs are done. Cool and serve.

MAKES 3 OR 4 SERVINGS

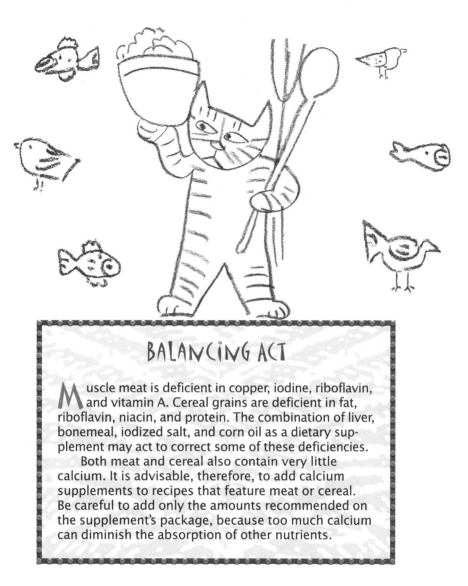

BALANCING ACT

Muscle meat is deficient in copper, iodine, riboflavin, and vitamin A. Cereal grains are deficient in fat, riboflavin, niacin, and protein. The combination of liver, bonemeal, iodized salt, and corn oil as a dietary supplement may act to correct some of these deficiencies.

Both meat and cereal also contain very little calcium. It is advisable, therefore, to add calcium supplements to recipes that feature meat or cereal. Be careful to add only the amounts recommended on the supplement's package, because too much calcium can diminish the absorption of other nutrients.

KITTY-SIZE LASAGNA

If you have a few noodles left over from making Sunday dinner, let your cat join in on the Italian feast.

A pinch of oregano
¼ clove garlic, minced
¼ teaspoon iodized salt
½ pound ground beef
1 lasagna noodle, cooked
½ cup tomato paste
1 teaspoon olive oil
¼ cup cottage cheese or ricotta cheese
1 teaspoon brewer's yeast
2 tablespoons grated cheddar cheese

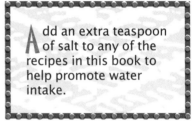

Add an extra teaspoon of salt to any of the recipes in this book to help promote water intake.

1. Add the oregano, garlic, and salt to the beef. Lightly brown in a skillet over medium heat.

2. Cut the cooked lasagna noodle into kitty-bite-size pieces. Add the noodle, tomato paste, and olive oil to the skillet and heat through.

3. Remove from heat, and mix in the cottage cheese and brewer's yeast. Top with grated cheddar cheese. Serve when cool.

MAKES 3 OR 4 SERVINGS

KITTY PIZZA

In a pizza parlor, this one might be called "everything-but-the-kitchen-sink."

  1 teaspoon corn oil
  ½ pound ground beef
  1 clove garlic, minced
  2 tablespoons finely chopped bell pepper
  1 tablespoon finely chopped olives
  1 tablespoon finely chopped mushrooms
  ½ teaspoon oregano
  1 teaspoon iodized salt
  ½ cup tomato puree (or ¼ cup tomato
    paste and ¼ cup water)
  2 tablespoons cooked liver (see page 4
    for instructions)
  ¼ cup grated mozzarella cheese
  ½ cup French bread, in small cubes
  2 tablespoons grated Parmesan cheese

1. Heat the oil in a skillet. Add the ground beef and lightly brown.

2. Add the garlic and sauté 1 minute. Add the bell pepper and sauté until soft. Add olives and mushrooms and sauté 2 minutes. Sprinkle with oregano and salt. Add the tomato puree and liver; simmer 2 to 3 minutes.

3. Turn heat to low and stir in the mozzarella cheese. Remove from heat when melted. Stir in the French bread and let cool.

4. Serve topped with Parmesan cheese.

MAKES 4 TO 6 SERVINGS

(ATS AND MiLK MiX...

Veterinary nutritionists caution against serving your cat a bowl of milk as a daily treat. Like people, cats can be lactose intolerant. This means that they lack the digestive enzyme lactase, and they cannot digest the lactose in milk. When they drink milk, lactose-intolerant cats may suffer from diarrhea, abdominal discomfort, and other problems.

If you feed dairy products to your cat, introduce them gradually. Give the cat small amounts (1 teaspoon) to start, and increase the volume (1 teaspoon at a time) over several weeks. Stop at the first sign of gastrointestinal upset.

. . . OR DO THEY?

Don't fret if your feline seems to be lactose intolerant; you need not limit the delicacies you set before him to only those that do not contain milk. Just substitute lactose-free milk or acidophilus milk (available at most health food stores) for the cow's milk. Your cat — and his belly — will be eminently pleased with the scrumptious treats.

BEEF AND BEAN SAUTÉ

With this easy recipe, it takes only a few minutes at the stove to create a tasty meat-and-vegetable dish.

>   1 tablespoon corn oil
>   1 clove garlic, minced
>   ½ pound ground beef
>   ⅓ cup finely chopped green beans
>   ½ teaspoon iodized salt
>   ⅓ cup cooked rice
>   1 tablespoon cooked liver (see page
>   4 for instructions)
>   ½ teaspoon bonemeal

1. Heat the oil in a skillet. Add the garlic and sauté approximately 30 seconds. Add the ground beef and cook until lightly browned.

2. Add the chopped green beans. Stir and continue cooking until the beans are soft.

3. Add the salt, rice, liver, and bonemeal, and toss until mixed well. Let cool and serve.

MAKES 4 TO 6 SERVINGS

KITTY TACO

Your cat will know it's time for a fiesta when she gets a taste of this version of a Mexican favorite.

½ pound ground beef
2 tablespoons finely chopped bell pepper
1 clove garlic, minced
1 tablespoon tomato paste
1 teaspoon corn oil
1 corn tortilla, cut into
   kitty-bite-size pieces
½ teaspoon bonemeal
½ teaspoon brewer's yeast
½ teaspoon iodized salt
2 tablespoons grated cheddar cheese

1. Start browning the ground beef over medium heat in a skillet.

2. When the meat is half cooked, add the bell pepper and garlic. Cook the mixture until the meat is golden brown.

3. Turn the heat to low. Stir in the tomato paste, corn oil, chopped tortilla, bonemeal, brewer's yeast, and salt. Stir until heated through.

4. Cool and serve topped with grated cheese.

MAKES 2 OR 3 SERVINGS

KITTY BATH
✳ ✳ ✳ ✳

Humans think a warm bath is divine; your cat may or may not agree. Follow this recipe for making the bathing experience as pleasant as possible for you and your kitty.

1 Kitty
1 grooming brush or comb
1 kitchen/utility sink or
   plastic basin
Warm water
1 towel or rubber mat
1 rubber or plastic cup

2 dry, warm towels
1 ounce of cat shampoo or
   baby's tearless shampoo

Optional:
 Crème rinse
 Hair dryer
 Mood music

1. Remove loose hair from the cat with a gentle combing or brushing.

2. Fill the sink or basin with 3 to 4 inches of warm water. Place a towel or rubber mat on the bottom to keep your cat from slipping.

3. Add one cat to the water. Using a large rubber or plastic cup, douse his or her head with warm water, then the rest of the body.

4. Squirt a line of shampoo down the full length of the cat. As you work the shampoo into a lather from head to tail, be very careful not to get soap in your cat's eyes or ears. To make long fur easier to comb after the bath, you may want to finish with a little crème rinse.

5. Give the cat a final rinse of warm, clean water to ensure that all shampoo residue is removed from the skin, which should prevent drying and irritation.

6. Wrap your cat in a warm towel and dry carefully. A second towel can be used to gently dry your pet thoroughly.

7. A hair dryer on the warm setting can be used to finish drying and fluffing — if your cat is still cooperating and hasn't decided to evacuate the scene posthaste.

KiTTY CHEESEBURGER

Does your cat give you that non-blinking begging stare whenever you munch on a burger with all the trimmings? Here's a healthy feline version that's easy to prepare.

    3 ounces ground beef
    2 tablespoons chicken broth
    3 tablespoons whole wheat
         bread crumbs
    1 egg
    1 small carrot, steamed and
         finely chopped
   ½ cup grated mozzarella cheese

1. In a medium-sized bowl, mash together the ground beef, chicken broth, bread crumbs, egg, and carrot.

2. Form the meaty mixture into two small burger patties.

3. Place the patties on a greased cookie sheet and broil the burgers until they are cooked through.

4. Remove the burgers from the oven and sprinkle the cheese on top.

5. Allow the cheese to melt and the burgers to cool. Serve patties one at a time, broken up into kitty-bite-size pieces.

MAKES 2 SERVINGS

MEWS AND PURRS MEAT LOAF

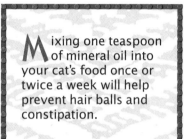

Fortify your feline on a chilly day with a dish of this warm goodness. This recipe makes a big enough batch that you can refrigerate the leftovers and serve them for a few days.

Mixing one teaspoon of mineral oil into your cat's food once or twice a week will help prevent hair balls and constipation.

½ pound ground beef
4 eggs
1½ cups whole wheat bread crumbs
2 cups milk
¼ cup peeled and shredded carrot
2 teaspoons bonemeal
2 tablespoons vegetable oil

1. Preheat oven to 350°F.

2. In a large mixing bowl, blend all the ingredients with a wooden spoon.

3. Put the mixture into a greased loaf pan.

4. Bake in the oven for 20 to 25 minutes.

5. Cool before serving. Refrigerate the leftovers in an airtight container.

MAKES 3 TO 5 SERVINGS

EGGS, CHEESE, AND MORE

A **little variety is important to you,** and it's important to your cat as well. As a change from their everyday diet, cats love the taste of a meaty meal or the smell of a fish dish, but they also can't resist a tempting bite of cheese. And as presented in the delicious recipes that follow, eggs, pasta, and greens will become some of your kitty's favorites.

Many people are now cutting back on the amount of meat in their meals for reasons of health, taste, and variety, so it makes sense that your cat's diet could follow this trend as well. Besides adding to the spice of life, the dishes here will provide essential nutrition for your cat. Eggs and cheese are packed with protein, pasta is an excellent source of carbo-hydrates, and greens provide vitamins and nutrients difficult to find else-where. Any diet — for your kitty or for yourself — needs to provide the proper amounts of protein, carbohydrates, fat, vitamins, and minerals. These mostly meatless meals contain that balance, and they can give your cat a break from the ho-hum everyday can o'cat chow.

WESTERN SCRAMBLE FOR KITTY ROUNDUPS

Saddle up for this tasty version of a classic hearty breakfast. It will look so good that you might even want to take a portion for yourself.

1 tablespoon margarine
¼ cup chopped ham or cooked ground beef
2 tablespoons chopped bell pepper
2 tablespoons chopped tomato
2 eggs
¼ teaspoon iodized salt
1 tablespoon milk or plain yogurt
2 tablespoons grated cheddar cheese
3 teaspoons sour cream
1 teaspoon brewer's yeast

1. Heat the margarine in a skillet. Add the meat, bell pepper, and tomato. Sauté until the bell pepper is soft.

2. Beat together the eggs, salt, and milk or yogurt. Add to the meat mixture. Add the cheese and scramble over low heat until the eggs are firm.

3. Top each portion with 1 teaspoon sour cream and a pinch of brewer's yeast.

MAKES 3 SERVINGS

68

KITTY ON THE RUN

Cats seem born to a life of unhurried luxury, spending their time lying in the sun and napping on the bed. Humans are generally quite the opposite. You'll appreciate this fast, no-cooking-required recipe when you want to make your cat a tasty dish in a jiffy.

⅓ cup cottage cheese
2 tablespoons Bisquick
1 tablespoon chopped cooked liver
  (see page 4 for instructions)
1 tablespoon corn oil
A dash of iodized salt

1. Mix all the ingredients thoroughly and serve.

2. Store any unused portions in an airtight container and refrigerate.

MAKES 1 OR 2 SERVINGS

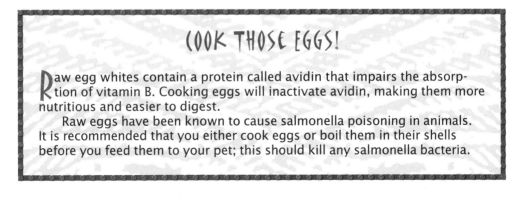

COOK THOSE EGGS!

Raw egg whites contain a protein called avidin that impairs the absorption of vitamin B. Cooking eggs will inactivate avidin, making them more nutritious and easier to digest.

Raw eggs have been known to cause salmonella poisoning in animals. It is recommended that you either cook eggs or boil them in their shells before you feed them to your pet; this should kill any salmonella bacteria.

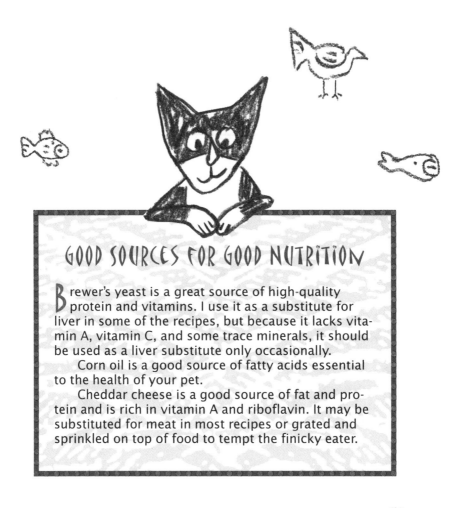

GOOD SOURCES FOR GOOD NUTRITION

Brewer's yeast is a great source of high-quality protein and vitamins. I use it as a substitute for liver in some of the recipes, but because it lacks vitamin A, vitamin C, and some trace minerals, it should be used as a liver substitute only occasionally.

Corn oil is a good source of fatty acids essential to the health of your pet.

Cheddar cheese is a good source of fat and protein and is rich in vitamin A and riboflavin. It may be substituted for meat in most recipes or grated and sprinkled on top of food to tempt the finicky eater.

CHEESE SCRAMBLE

These scrambled eggs have tasty cheddar cheese as well as healthy sprouts. Make sure the sprouts you use are fresh and carefully washed.

- 3 eggs
- 3 tablespoons grated cheddar cheese
- 2 tablespoons milk or plain yogurt
- 2 tablespoons sprouts
- 1 teaspoon brewer's yeast
- ½ teaspoon iodized salt
- 1 tablespoon margarine

1. Mix all the ingredients except the margarine in a medium-sized bowl.

2. Heat the margarine in a skillet until melted. Add the egg mixture. Scramble over low heat until the eggs are cooked.

3. Cool and serve.

MAKES 2 OR 3 SERVINGS

KITTY FONDUE

Don't worry, you don't really have to teach your cat how to handle those little fondue forks for her to enjoy this cheesy delight.

   1 teaspoon corn oil
   1 clove garlic, minced
   1 cup grated cheddar cheese
   ½ cup condensed cream of chicken soup
   ½ teaspoon iodized salt
   ¼ cup chicken broth
   2 tablespoons cooked liver (see
       page 4 for instructions)
   1 cup of kitty-bite-size
       pieces of French bread

1. Heat the oil in a saucepan. Add the garlic and sauté 1 minute.

2. Add the cheese, soup, and salt. Stir constantly over low heat until the cheese has melted and the mixture is creamy.

3. Remove from heat and stir in the chicken broth and liver.

4. When the mixture has cooled to lukewarm, stir in the French bread and serve.

MAKES 3 OR 4 SERVINGS

KITTY MEDICINE CHEST

It is a good idea to keep a few items on hand for treating your cat's minor health problems. However, if a condition persists for more than a day or two, consult your vet immediately.

If your pet has diarrhea, treat it with Kaopectate. Using a plastic eyedropper, administer one teaspoon as often as five times a day. If the diarrhea continues for more than one day, call your veterinarian.

Your cat may run a fever for many reasons. Symptoms that may accompany a fever include listlessness, lack of appetite, vomiting, or diarrhea. You can use a rectal thermometer to check the temperature of your pet. A cat's normal temperature is between 100.5°F and 102°F. If your cat has a temperature higher than 102°, call your veterinarian.

An antiseptic ointment that is suitable for small children is also useful for treating minor cuts and scrapes on your cat.

GRASSY GOODNESS

Many cats love to munch on some greens now and then. They'll consider this salad a real treat, and it's a snap to make.

1 small carrot, peeled and finely grated
½ cup chopped sprouts
2 teaspoons finely chopped fresh parsley
½ teaspoon fresh organic catnip
2 tablespoons vegetable broth

1. Blend the vegetables and herbs in a medium-sized bowl.

2. Add the vegetable broth and lightly toss.

3. Serve a small portion in your cat's bowl and store the leftovers in an airtight container in the refrigerator.

MAKES 2 OR 3 SERVINGS

HERBS FOR YOUR CAT

More than ever, people are cooking with herbs and using them as physical remedies and dietary supplements. Your cat could also benefit from something more than an occasional pinch of catnip. For a specific medical condition, you should consult with your veterinarian before treating with herbs, especially if your cat is taking prescription drugs. But there are a number of gentle herbs that you can use on a regular basis to help enhance your cat's immune system and promote overall good health.

Besides the ever-popular catnip, good herbs to give your cat include burdock (for improving skin conditions), caraway and dill (for soothing the stomach), echinacea (for boosting the immune system), and parsley (for alleviating bladder problems and as a nutritional supplement). Fresh or dried herbs can be chopped fine, with a pinch mixed into your cat's regular food. You can also make an herbal tea to pour over your cat's meal or add to his water bowl. To make a tea, steep 1 or 2 teaspoons of dried herbs or 2 to 4 tablespoons of fresh herbs in a cup of hot water for 10 to 15 minutes and then strain. For smaller cats, add ⅛ cup of herbal tea to their diet once or twice a day; larger cats can have up to ¼ cup. You should consult a veterinarian, though, before giving any herbs to kittens, to pregnant or nursing cats, or to cats taking prescription drugs.

As another serving idea, why not serve up your cat's meal with a sprig of parsley as a garnish? Parsley is packed with nutrition and has a "green" taste that most cats enjoy. While you're at it, make sure you put a sprig on your own plate. It is always good to set a healthy example, whether it's for your kids or your kitty.

A KiTTY GiFT BAG

One great thing about giving your cat a toy or treat in a decorated gift bag: No matter what the cat thinks of the present, there's always an empty bag left over to bat around and hide in. It's as surefire a trick as giving a toddler a gift packaged in a large cardboard box. Here's how to make a special bag for your feline friend:

1. Toss a pinch of catnip in the bottom of a brown paper bag.

2. Place the gift item, loosely wrapped in tissue paper, inside the bag.

3. Lightly fold the top of bag closed so that your cat can help you open it up and discover what's inside.

PURR-FECT PASTA

Bring out the Italian in your frisky feline with this easy-to-make pasta dish. Your cat will howl, "Meow-a Mia! That's great pasta!"

- 1 cup uncooked macaroni pasta
- 1 tablespoon olive oil
- 1 egg
- ¼ cup milk
- ¼ cup grated cheddar cheese

1. In a small saucepan, bring the macaroni pasta to a boil. Reduce the heat and allow the noodles to simmer for 7 to 10 minutes. Drain the pasta and pour into a medium bowl. Set aside.

2. In a medium-sized frying pan, warm the olive oil over low heat.

3. Stir in the egg and milk and cook, stirring constantly, until the eggs are firm. Remove from heat.

4. Combine the egg and milk mixture with the pasta.

5. Sprinkle on the cheddar cheese.

6. Cool and serve.

MAKES 2 OR 3 SERVINGS

TANDEM COOKING

Let's face it: You may have a great time preparing the recipes in the preceding chapters as occasional treats for your kitty, but making a homemade meal takes some time — something that is always in short supply. It can be hard enough to find the time and energy to put together a home-cooked dinner for yourself and your family, even without having to make an entirely separate dish for the feline member of the household.

That's where the Tandem Cooking recipes come to the rescue. First, you use the main part of the recipe to make a delicious dinner for your family — and maybe some guests, too. Then, with a few adjustments or additions, you can easily turn part of the dinner into a meal for your cat, with just the ingredients and nutritional balance that she needs. Everyone can eat the same meal together — what better way to make your kitty know she is part of the family?

Keep in mind that the recipes should be followed just as written, at least for the part of the meal you are going to put in the cat bowl. You may consider recipes just the starting point for your creativity, but your cat needs a meal with the ingredients and proportions that are right for her. After you set aside part of the main recipe for the kitty version, feel free to spice up the people servings as you wish.

As a timesaving measure, each of these recipes will make enough for two or three kitty servings, so you'll have enough for another meal or two. With such delicious favorites as Shish Kebab and Chicken Cordon Bleu, you won't have to worry about what to do with the leftover people servings. There won't be any.

BEEF STROGANOFF

These strips of beef in a creamy sauce served over rice — or noodles if you prefer — are certain to please cat, owner, and guests alike. *Note:* Onions are for human consumption only. Follow the steps, and don't stir the onions back into the kitty portions.

For People
      2 pounds beef tenderloin
      8 tablespoons butter
      2 medium onions, sliced fine
     16 mushrooms, sliced fine
     1½ cups sour cream
    Salt and pepper

1. Cut the beef into ½-inch by 2-inch strips.

2. Melt 2 tablespoons of the butter in a skillet. Add the onions and sauté until they are golden brown. Remove the onions from skillet.

3. Add 1 tablespoon of butter to the skillet. Add the mushrooms and sauté for about 5 minutes. Remove the mushrooms from the skillet and set aside.

4. Heat the remaining butter in the skillet until it is bubbling. Add half of the beef and quickly brown on all sides, about 5 minutes. Remove the cooked beef and brown the remaining beef.

5. Put the beef and mushrooms back into the skillet and stir to heat through. Add salt and pepper to taste. Stir in the sour cream. Remove kitty portions.

6. Stir in the onions. Heat until it nearly boils. Serve immediately over rice.

MAKES 6 PEOPLE SERVINGS OR
4 PEOPLE SERVINGS AND 2 OR 3 KITTY SERVINGS

For Kitty

⅔ cup Beef Stroganoff
(set aside before the onions
were stirred back in)
⅓ cup cooked rice
1 teaspoon brewer's yeast

1. Chop the stroganoff into kitty-bite-size pieces.

2. Combine the stroganoff, rice, and brewer's yeast, and stir well. Serve cool.

MAKES 2 OR 3 SERVINGS

SHISH KEBAB

Aperfect summer barbecue dish, shish kebab allows you to pick and choose among a wide variety of ingredients. When assembling the skewers, put elements that will need to cook a little longer, like thick vegetable slices, and elements that cook more quickly, like fruit, on separate skewers. *Note:* Pearl onions and garlic cloves are for the People portions only.

For People
2 to 2½ pounds lamb, boneless shoulder,
    boneless rib, or loin chops

Vegetable suggestions (choose any or all):
Bell pepper, cut into squares
Garlic cloves
Mushroom caps
Pearl onions
Tomato, quartered (or cherry tomatoes)
Zucchini, 1-inch-thick slices, halved

Fruit suggestions (choose any or all):
Apple chunks
Banana, thick slices
Cantaloupe or honeydew melon chunks
Lime or orange chunks
Pineapple chunks, fresh or canned (canned
    will provide juice for the marinade)
Spiced crabapples, whole

1. Cut the meat into 1- or 1½-inch cubes. Place in a bowl or deep dish and pour in enough marinade to cover the meat. Lift and separate the pieces so that all sides of the cubes are coated with marinade. Let stand in refrigerator at least 2 hours, or overnight.

2. After the meat has marinated, combine it with the vegetables and fruit on skewers. Be creative with combinations.

3. Place the skewers on a hot barbecue or under a broiler. Turn and baste with the reserved marinade as necessary, until the meat is done to your taste and the kebabs are browned evenly. Keep an eye on the kebabs while cooking, as they can burn quickly.

MAKES 6 PEOPLE SERVINGS OR 4 PEOPLE SERVINGS AND
2 OR 3 KITTY SERVINGS

Marinade
1½ cups soy sauce
1 cup wine vinegar
1 cup pineapple juice
¾ cup brown sugar
1 teaspoon salt

1. Combine the ingredients in a mixing bowl and stir well. Use as a marinade for the meat.

2. Reserve leftover marinade in the refrigerator to use as a basting sauce.

MAKES ABOUT 4 CUPS

KITTY KEBAB

Once you've grilled all the shish kebab ingredients for family and friends, it's a snap to put together this dish for kitty.

4 Shish Kebab lamb cubes chopped into kitty-bite-size pieces or ground
¼ cup Shish Kebab vegetables (except the pearl onions and garlic cloves)
⅓ cup cooked white rice
1 teaspoon corn oil
½ teaspoon iodized salt
1 teaspoon bonemeal
2 tablespoons cooked liver (see page 4 for instructions)
2 tablespoons Shish Kebab Marinade

Combine all the ingredients in a mixing bowl. Stir until well blended. Serve cool.

MAKES 2 OR 3 SERVINGS

SAFE AT HOME

It is a good idea to "cat proof" your house, for the sake of both your feline and your finances. Damage can result to both pet and property unless precautions are taken.

■ If your cat likes to perch on window ledges, be sure that the windows and screens are secure.

■ Keep small objects and potted plants picked up and well out of reach. An adventurous cat may try to eat anything that is small enough or easily accessible.

■ Electrical cords to lamps, televisions, and appliances should be concealed as much as possible. Your cat may try to play with any loose cord and end up pulling down a lamp or appliance, or he may seriously burn, or even electrocute, himself. Unplug all cords to nonessential or unused electrical appliances, and don't leave them dangling. This is especially important if you are leaving your pet alone in the house for a few days.

CHICKEN PAPRIKA
▽△▽△▽△▽

Paprika is made of dried, ground sweet peppers — not those fiery habañeros — but you should still consider adjusting the amount you use, based on how much taste you and your cat have for spiciness.

For People
1 tablespoon corn oil
1 teaspoon iodized salt
2 tablespoons paprika
1 cup hot water
1 3-pound chicken, skinned, boned, and cut into bite-size pieces
1 carrot, chopped fine
2 medium potatoes, cut into small cubes
½ cup chicken broth
2 tomatoes, chopped
1 red bell pepper, chopped fine
1 green bell pepper, chopped fine
Fresh parsley

1. Warm the oil in a 4-quart saucepan over medium heat. Add the salt, paprika, and ½ cup of the hot water to the pan. Cover and simmer over low heat for 10 minutes.

2. Add the chicken and the rest of water, then simmer another 20 minutes. Add the carrot, potatoes, and chicken broth. Simmer for 10 minutes.

WATER, WATER EVERYWHERE

Water should be available to your cat at all times. Some cats prefer fresh water; others simply want their dish topped off each day. Whatever your cat prefers is best — a healthy allowance of water every day will help prevent health problems.

88

3. Add the tomato and red and green bell pepper to the pan. Stir well and simmer 10 more minutes. Garnish with fresh parsley and serve.

MAKES 6 PEOPLE SERVINGS OR 4 PEOPLE SERVINGS AND
2 OR 3 KITTY SERVINGS

For Kitty

1 cup Chicken Paprika
¼ cup cooked rice
½ teaspoon brewer's yeast
½ teaspoon bonemeal

1. Chop the Chicken Paprika into kitty-bite-size pieces.

2. Mix the rice, brewer's yeast, and bonemeal with the Chicken Paprika. Serve cool.

MAKES 2 OR 3 SERVINGS

SALMON LOAF

Using canned salmon makes this dish easy to prepare anytime; adding the Dill Sauce makes it a delight to eat.

For People
1 12-ounce can salmon, skinned, boned, and drained
½ cup evaporated skimmed milk
2 slices white bread, cut into small cubes
2 eggs, slightly beaten
¼ cup finely chopped celery
½ teaspoon dill
1 teaspoon lemon juice
¼ teaspoon thyme
A dash of salt and pepper
1 tablespoon melted butter

1. Preheat oven to 350°F.

2. Combine all the ingredients except the butter in a medium-sized mixing bowl and stir well. Fold in the melted butter.

3. Grease an 8½-by-4½-by-2½-inch glass loaf pan, spoon in the salmon mixture, and smooth the top.

4. Bake for 35 to 45 minutes, or until the loaf is firm in the center.

5. Loosen from the sides of the pan with a spatula and invert onto a serving platter. Serve plain or with Dill Sauce.

MAKES 4 PEOPLE SERVINGS OR 3 PEOPLE SERVINGS
AND 1 OR 2 KITTY SERVINGS

Dill Sauce

1 cup sour cream or plain yogurt
⅔ cup peeled, seeded, and
    finely chopped cucumber
2 tablespoons sugar
1 tablespoon Dijon mustard
1 tablespoon dill weed
1 tablespoon white wine vinegar
½ teaspoon salt

Combine all the ingredients and refrigerate for 30 minutes before serving.

For Kitty

⅔ cup Salmon Loaf, cooled
½ teaspoon bonemeal, or
    half of the bones removed
    from the canned salmon if
    they are soft
½ teaspoon brewer's yeast

1. Break up the Salmon Loaf into kitty-bite-size pieces.

2. Mix in the bonemeal or salmon bones (if soft) and the brewer's yeast. Serve cool.

MAKES 1 OR 2 SERVINGS

RABBIT STEW

♥ ♥ ♥ ♥ ♥

Rabbit doesn't usually make its way onto our dinner tables (or into our cat's bowl), but this is a traditional recipe that is definitely worth trying.

For People

 2 2½- to 3-pound rabbits, boned
    and cut into bite-size pieces
Salt and pepper
½ cup flour
½ pound bacon, sliced
½ cup red wine
1½ cups chicken broth
 2 tablespoons sherry (optional)
⅛ teaspoon rosemary
⅛ teaspoon thyme

1. Season the rabbit pieces with salt and pepper to taste and dredge in flour.

2. Fry the bacon until crisp; drain, crumble, and reserve the drippings. Heat the bacon drippings in a large pan or skillet. Add the rabbit pieces and brown. Set aside.

3. Drain all but 2 tablespoons of the bacon drippings from the pan. Add the wine and chicken broth and bring to a boil, stirring constantly to deglaze the pan.

4. Stir in the rest of the ingredients, including the crumbled bacon. Add the rabbit pieces, cover, and simmer for 1 hour.

MAKES 6 PEOPLE SERVINGS OR 4 PEOPLE SERVINGS AND 2 OR 3 KITTY SERVINGS

For Kitty
1 cup Rabbit Stew
½ cup cooked rice
1 tablespoon cooked liver (see page 4 for instructions)
½ teaspoon bonemeal
½ teaspoon iodized salt
1 teaspoon corn oil

1. Chop the Rabbit Stew into kitty-bite-size pieces.

2. Combine all the ingredients in a mixing bowl and stir thoroughly. Serve cool.

MAKES 2 OR 3 SERVINGS

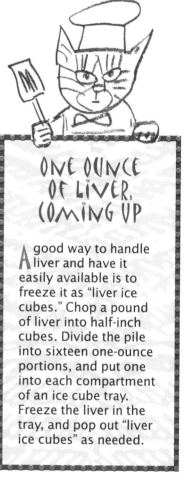

ONE OUNCE OF LIVER, COMING UP

A good way to handle liver and have it easily available is to freeze it as "liver ice cubes." Chop a pound of liver into half-inch cubes. Divide the pile into sixteen one-ounce portions, and put one into each compartment of an ice cube tray. Freeze the liver in the tray, and pop out "liver ice cubes" as needed.

95

CHICKEN CORDON BLEU

Another traditional dish, this combination of chicken, ham, and Swiss cheese is a real crowd-pleaser.

For People

- 5 tablespoons chopped ham
- 5 tablespoons grated Swiss cheese
- 1 tablespoon white wine
- 5 boneless chicken breast halves (1 for your cat)
- ⅓ cup flour
- ½ teaspoon iodized salt
- A dash of white pepper
- 1 large egg
- ¼ cup plus 1 teaspoon corn oil
- ⅓ cup dried bread crumbs
- 4 tablespoons butter

1. Mix the ham and cheese with the white wine. Divide the ham and cheese mixture into five equal portions. Reserve one portion for your cat.

2. Place 4 chicken breasts skin side down and spread a portion of the ham and cheese mixture over each breast. Roll up each breast and tie closed with string or secure with toothpicks. Refrigerate for 20 to 30 minutes.

3. Combine the flour, salt, and white pepper, and dredge each chicken breast with the flour mixture. Beat the egg with 1 teaspoon corn oil. Carefully brush each breast with the egg mixture. Roll each breast in bread crumbs.

4. Heat ¼ cup of the corn oil and the butter in a skillet. Fry the chicken breasts until golden brown and cooked through (10 to 15 minutes per side over medium-low heat). Drain and serve.

MAKES 4 PEOPLE SERVINGS AND
2 OR 3 KITTY SERVINGS

For Kitty

1 tablespoon butter
1 chicken breast (with skin), chopped into kitty-bite-size pieces
1 portion Chicken Cordon Bleu ham and cheese mixture
⅓ cup cooked rice
½ teaspoon bonemeal
½ teaspoon brewer's yeast

For kitties, warm food is more palatable than cold food. When you rewarm food for cats, you must treat it like baby food: Test the temperature on the skin of your inner forearm, and before serving, check for hot spots that might burn your kitty's tongue.

1. Heat the butter in a skillet. Lightly brown the chopped chicken.

2. Over low heat, stir in the ham and cheese mixture and the rice. Stir until heated through.

3. Remove from heat and stir in the bonemeal and brewer's yeast. Serve cool. Store unused portions in an airtight container in the refrigerator.

MAKES 2 OR 3 KITTY SERVINGS

SPECIAL DIETS

We all know people on special diets. Those with high blood pressure avoid foods high in sodium; those who want to lose a few pounds count calories; and expectant mothers take extra care to eat a nutritious and well-balanced diet.

Cats and dogs have health problems similar to those of people and, like people, sometimes need to follow a modified diet that is different from that of the average pet.

Your veterinarian may recommend a special diet for your pet when there are indications that it is necessary. Perhaps your cat has a food-related allergy or an intestinal disability. Maybe she's stubbornly overweight, or she could have a chronic kidney or liver disorder. Your cat may even be troubled with urinary stoppages. A special diet can help considerably. The following pages explain how the various diets are planned and how they can help.

Every pet deserves to see a veterinarian at least once a year to check immunities and evaluate overall physical condition. When your pet has a condition requiring a special diet, regular visits to the vet are even more important. Even when your pet appears to be in good health, be sure you do your part to help him or her have a happy, long life by providing regular medical care and a healthy diet.

SPECIAL INSTRUCTIONS FOR SPECIAL DIETS

The recipes that follow are designed for cats with particular dietary needs. They were developed by veterinary nutritionist Mark L. Morris, Jr., D.V.M., Ph.D., and were first published in a book that Dr. Morris co-authored with Dr. Lon D. Lewis entitled *Small Animal Clinical Nutrition*. This textbook is recognized as an authoritative source on small animal nutrition and is used in schools of veterinary medicine throughout the world. The most recent edition of this book, *Small Animal Clinical Nutrition, Fourth Edition,* is published by the Mark Morris Institute in Topeka, Kansas, and the recipes are reprinted here by permission.

These recipes were originally based on the Hill's Pet Prescription Diets first developed by Dr. Morris's father, Dr. Mark Morris, Sr., a noted pioneer in pet nutrition. If you would like more information about pet nutrition, or if you are interested in obtaining commercially produced prescription diet products, you can visit the Web site of Hill's Pet Nutrition at www.hillspet.com or call them at (800) 445-5777.

Note: These recipes are so specialized that they are not recommended for cats that are generally healthy. If you suspect that your cat has a health problem that would require a special diet, please consult your veterinarian before starting your pet on one of these dietary programs.

SWITCHING TO A NEW FOOD

For maximum health benefit, you want to start feeding your cat the recommended prescription diet as soon as possible. However, an abrupt switch isn't always advisable. The new food may be quite different in digestive properties than your cat's current diet, so start off with a smaller portion than the amount recommended, mixing it in with an adjusted amount of your cat's normal feed. Give your cat time to get accustomed to the new food, and gradually increase the quantity up to the amount recommended.

Real Food

FOR FOOD-RELATED ALLERGIES

If your veterinarian suspects that a food allergy is causing problems for your cat, such as hives (which you may have mistaken for fleas) or diarrhea, he or she may recommend a shift to a hypoallergenic diet as the simplest way to determine if your cat's problems are allergy related.

A nutritionally balanced meal, the allergy diet is made with hypoallergenic ingredients. If your cat's symptoms are relieved after a period of time on this diet, your veterinarian will know that the cat's ailment is related to a food allergy. The veterinarian will suggest the next step. In some cases, the simplest and most effective course is to feed the allergy diet as the exclusive diet for the remainder of your cat's life.

ALLERGY DIET

If you suspect that an allergy is food related, maintain your cat on a diet of the allergy diet and distilled water. Then expose the patient to various foods, one at a time, to discover the offending products. Begin with tap water, and watch your animal closely for any aggravating symptoms. The aim of this provocative exposure to all kinds of foods is to determine what your cat *can* eat, rather than what he or she cannot eat.

¼ pound diced lamb
1 cup cooked white rice
1 teaspoon corn oil
1½ teaspoons dicalcium phosphate

1. Trim any fat from the lamb.

2. Cook the lamb thoroughly (braise or roast) without seasoning. Add the remaining ingredients and mix well.

3. Keep covered in the refrigerator.

MAKES ¾ POUND

FEEDING GUIDE FOR CATS ON AN ALLERGY DIET

Feed your cat an amount sufficient to maintain normal body weight.

BODY WEIGHT	APPROXIMATE DAILY FEEDING
5 pounds	¼ pound
7 to 8 pounds	⅓ pound
10 pounds	⅖ pound

FOR A DELICATE INTESTINE

ntestinal upsets stem from a variety of causes. Sometimes a cat ingests highly irritating material or has an intestinal infection. A few cats have an unusually sensitive intestinal tract, just as humans may have chronic colitis. In these situations, a bland, nonirritating, and easily digested diet is necessary.

Nutritious and highly digestible, the soft, bland diet is made from ingredients unlikely to irritate the intestines. It is often used for cats recovering from abdominal surgery. It can also be used to aid in recovery from diarrhea that is sometimes accompanied by a loss of appetite. Because it is so easily digested and soft, the soft, bland diet may be prescribed for kittens until their digestive tracts are fully developed As a diet, it places minimum stress on your cat's digestive organs and supplies the nutrients needed for growth, as for well as healing and tissue repair.

SOFT, BLAND DIET

½ cup Cream of Wheat
1½ cups creamed cottage cheese
1 large hard-boiled egg
2 tablespoons brewer's yeast
3 tablespoons granulated sugar
1 tablespoon corn oil
1 tablespoon potassium chloride
2 teaspoons dicalcium phosphate
Balanced vitamin-mineral supplement
   (available from your vet
   or pet store)

1. Cook the Cream of Wheat according to the package directions. Cool.

2. Add the remaining ingredients and mix well.

3. Keep covered in the refrigerator.

MAKES 2 POUNDS

FEEDING GUIDE FOR CATS ON A SOFT, BLAND DIET

Feed your cat an amount sufficient to maintain normal body weight.

BODY WEIGHT	APPROXIMATE DAILY FEEDING
5 pounds	¼ pound
7 to 8 pounds	⅓ pound
10 pounds	⅖ pound

FOR OBESITY

Excessive weight can make your cat uncomfortable. It can also shorten his or her life. The overweight cat may have difficulty exercising or even breathing. Bone structure may be sorely strained and arthritis can result. Excess fat may hinder the proper functioning of the heart, liver, or digestive tract.

Reducing your cat's ration of regular food is not the best solution; when you reduce amounts enough to cut calories, you also reduce essential proteins, vitamins, and minerals necessary for good health.

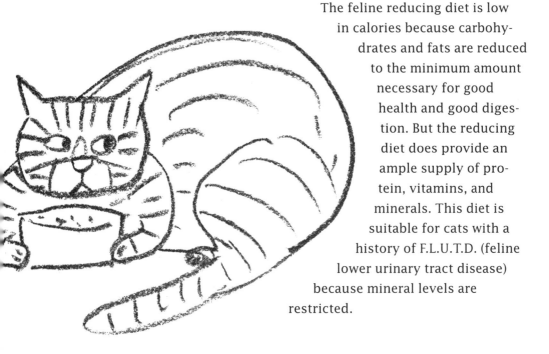

The feline reducing diet is low in calories because carbohydrates and fats are reduced to the minimum amount necessary for good health and good digestion. But the reducing diet does provide an ample supply of protein, vitamins, and minerals. This diet is suitable for cats with a history of F.L.U.T.D. (feline lower urinary tract disease) because mineral levels are restricted.

REDUCING DIET
♡ ♡ ♡ ♡ ♡

Snacking and scavenging should be absolutely forbidden during the reducing period. After the cat attains an ideal weight, a quality diet at a level that just maintains that weight can be initiated.

1½ pounds pork liver, cooked
    and ground
1 cup cooked rice
1 teaspoon cooking oil
1 teaspoon calcium carbonate

1. Combine all the ingredients.

2. Keep covered in the refrigerator.

MAKES 1¾ POUNDS

FEEDING GUIDE
FOR CATS ON A
REDUCING DIET

BODY WEIGHT	APPROXIMATE DAILY FEEDING
5 pounds	¼ pound
7 to 8 pounds	⅓ pound
10 pounds	½ pound

FOR IMPAIRED LIVER AND KIDNEY FUNCTION

ats, like dogs and other creatures, can suffer from kidney disorders. The normal kidney helps the body eliminate wastes from food proteins. If the proteins are of excellent quality, the kidneys don't need to work as hard to process the waste products generated by food proteins. Too much protein in a diet can strain diseased kidneys. Therefore, the amount of protein in a cat's diet should be reduced if he or she is suffering from weakened kidneys. Whatever protein a cat does eat should be of a higher quality.

The feline kidney diet is a superior nutritional food made with specially selected and carefully balanced proteins. It may be fed to a cat over a long period of time. No additional food should be offered to a cat with ailing or diseased kidneys — serious illness could result.

FELINE KIDNEY DIET

This recipe provides a balanced diet that should be served in a quantity sufficient to provide the daily requirements for each vitamin and trace mineral.

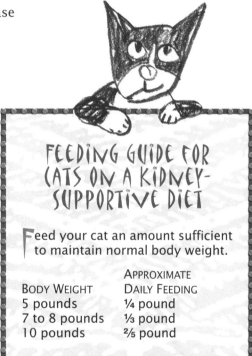

- 1 tablespoon fat (bacon grease or cooking oil)
- ¼ pound cooked liver (see page 4 for instructions)
- 1 large egg, hard-boiled
- 2 cups cooked white rice
- 1 teaspoon calcium carbonate

1. Warm the fat in a skillet. Add the liver and brown. Do not drain the fat.

2. Dice or grind the liver and the egg. Combine all the ingredients and mix well. This mixture is somewhat dry, but the palatability may be improved by adding some water (not milk).

MAKES 1¼ POUNDS

FEEDING GUIDE FOR CATS ON A KIDNEY-SUPPORTIVE DIET

Feed your cat an amount sufficient to maintain normal body weight.

BODY WEIGHT	APPROXIMATE DAILY FEEDING
5 pounds	¼ pound
7 to 8 pounds	⅓ pound
10 pounds	⅖ pound

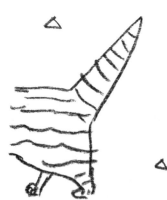

FOR URINARY STOPPAGES

The bodies of some cats cannot manage mineral matter properly. (On ordinary pet food labels, mineral matter may be referred to as "ash.") Mineral crystals in the bladder or urethra gather together to form larger units called calculuses, gravel, or stones. The presence of this matter can cause pain during urination, blood in the urine, and even retention of urine (which can cause blood poisoning).

The feline restricted-mineral diet is different from ordinary cat food in that its mineral content is only the amount necessary for proper nutrition. Hence, there is less mineral matter available in your cat's system to encourage stone formation. In addition, it is high in protein, fat, vitamin A, and B-complex vitamins, and it is easily digested by the body.

RESTRICTED-MINERAL DIET FOR URINARY STOPPAGES

For this diet to be effective, make sure that no supplementary parts of your cat's diet are adding mineral material.

> 1 pound ground beef, cooked
> ¼ pound pork liver, cooked
> 1 cup cooked white rice
> 1 teaspoon corn oil
> 1 teaspoon calcium carbonate

1. Combine all the ingredients.

2. Store covered in the refrigerator.

MAKES 1¾ POUNDS

FEEDING GUIDE FOR CATS ON A RESTRICTED-MINERAL DIET

Feed your cat an amount sufficient to maintain normal body weight.

BODY WEIGHT	APPROXIMATE DAILY FEEDING
5 pounds	⅕ pound
7 to 8 pounds	¼ pound
10 pounds	⅓ pound

113

INDEX

Meat loaf, 65
Medical care, 99
Medicines, 75. *See also* Herbs
Milk, 58–59
Mineral matter, 112
Mineral oil, for hair ball prevention, 65
Morris, Mark L. Jr., 100
Morris, Mark L. Sr., 100

Noodles. *See* Pasta
Nursing cats, 77

Obesity, 106–7

Paprika, 88–89
Parsley, 76, 77
Pasta
   in chicken dishes, 36, 37, 42
   in fish dishes, 18
   lasagna, 56
   macaroni and cheese, 79
Petroleum jelly, for hair ball
   prevention, 38
Pizza, 57
Plants, safety and, 87
Popsicles, 8
Pork, 48
Potassium chloride, 105
Potato, 4
Poultry. *See* Chicken; Turkey
Pregnancy, 77
Protein, 51. *See also specific types*

Rabbit, 94–95
Reducing diet, 107
Refrigeration of foods, 3
Restricted-mineral diet, 112–13
Riboflavin, 72
Rice
   substitutions for, 4

Safety, 3, 23, 31, 47, 69,
   77, 87, 97
Salads, 33
Salmon, 4, 90–91
Salmonella poisoning, 5, 69
Salt, 2, 51, 53, 56
Sardines, 24, 29
Scrapes, treating, 75
Seafood. *See* Fish and seafood
Shish kebab, 84–85
Shrimp, 19, 27
Soft, bland diet, 104–5
Sole, 18
Soups and stews
   chicken, 19, 37, 41
   fish, 19, 25, 29
   meat, 19, 49, 51, 94–95
Sprouts, 73, 76
Stews. *See* Soups and stews
Stones, 112
Supplements
   for cereals, 51, 53
   in Kronfeld recipe, 2
   for meat, 53
   vitamin-mineral, 105
Sushi, 26

Tacos, 28, 61
Tapioca, 4
Temperature, normal, 75
Thiaminase, 17
Thiamine, 17
Tortillas, 28, 61
Trout, 13
Tuna, 8, 23, 26
Turkey, 4, 43, 45

Urinary stoppages, 112–13

METRIC CONVERSION CHART

Conversions between U.S. and metric measurements will be somewhat inexact, unless you have very precise measuring equipment. Be sure to convert the measurements for all of the ingredients in a recipe to maintain the same proportions as the original.

GENERAL FORMULAS FOR METRIC CONVERSION

Ounces to grams	multiply ounces by 28.35
Pounds to grams	multiply pounds by 453.5
Pounds to kilograms	multiply pounds by 0.45
Cups to liters	multiply cups by 0.24
Fahrenheit to Celsius	subtract 32 from Fahrenheit temperature, multiply by 5, then divide by 9

APPROXIMATE METRIC EQUIVALENTS BY VOLUME

U.S.	METRIC
1 teaspoon	5 milliliters
1 tablespoon	15 milliliters
¼ cup	60 milliliters
½ cup	120 milliliters
1 cup	230 milliliters
2 cups	460 milliliters
4 cups (1 quart)	0.95 liter

OTHER STOREY TITLES YOU WILL ENJOY

50 Simple Ways to Pamper Your Cat, by Arden Moore.
All the grooming, socializing, feeding, and playing tips to make your cat feel like a king.
144 pages. Paper. ISBN-13: 978-1-58017-311-7.

50 Simple Ways to Pamper Your Dog, by Arden Moore.
No-fuss tips to feed, groom, play with, and socialize your dog into health and happiness.
144 pages. Paper. ISBN-13: 978-1-58017-310-0.

The Cat Behavior Answer Book, by Arden Moore.
Practical insights into the feline mind — for cat owners everywhere!
336 pages. Paper. ISBN-13: 978-1-58017-674-3.

Dr. Kidd's Guide to Herbal Cat Care, by Randy Kidd, DVM, PhD.
Thorough information on using all-natural herbal remedies to treat and prevent disease in your favorite feline.
208 pages. Paper. ISBN-13: 978-1-58017-188-5.

The Kitten Owner's Manual, by Arden Moore.
Solutions to all your kitten quandaries, from a cat expert.
208 pages. Paper. ISBN-13: 978-1-58017-387-2.

Real Food for Dogs, by Arden Moore.
A collection of 50 vet-approved recipes to please your canine gastronome.
128 pages. Paper. ISBN-13: 978-1-58017-424-4.

These and other books from Storey Publishing are available wherever quality books are sold or by calling 1-800-441-5700.
Visit us at *www.storey.com*.